this book belongs to

a Paul Doodles original

Time to get a new notebook

www.ingramcontent.com/pod-product-compliance
Lightning Source LLC
Chambersburg PA
CBHW081602220526
45468CB00010B/2739
9781798273210